# Oriental scenery. Twenty-four views in Hindoostan, taken in the years 1789 and 1790; drawn and engraved by Thomas Daniell, ...

## Thomas Daniell

ECCO
PRINT EDITIONS

*Oriental scenery. Twenty-four views in Hindoostan, taken in the years 1789 and 1790; drawn and engraved by Thomas Daniell, ...*
Daniell, Thomas
ESTCID: T147411
Reproduction from British Library
The plates were issued separately and are dated 1795, 1796, and 1797. Printer's name from the plates. With a half-title.
London : March 1 [printed by Robert Bowyer], 1795 [1797]
28p.,XXIV plates ; 8°

## Gale ECCO Print Editions

Relive history with *Eighteenth Century Collections Online*, now available in print for the independent historian and collector. This series includes the most significant English-language and foreign-language works printed in Great Britain during the eighteenth century, and is organized in seven different subject areas including literature and language; medicine, science, and technology; and religion and philosophy. The collection also includes thousands of important works from the Americas.

The eighteenth century has been called "The Age of Enlightenment." It was a period of rapid advance in print culture and publishing, in world exploration, and in the rapid growth of science and technology – all of which had a profound impact on the political and cultural landscape. At the end of the century the American Revolution, French Revolution and Industrial Revolution, perhaps three of the most significant events in modern history, set in motion developments that eventually dominated world political, economic, and social life.

In a groundbreaking effort, Gale initiated a revolution of its own: digitization of epic proportions to preserve these invaluable works in the largest online archive of its kind. Contributions from major world libraries constitute over 175,000 original printed works. Scanned images of the actual pages, rather than transcriptions, recreate the works *as they first appeared.*

Now for the first time, these high-quality digital scans of original works are available via print-on-demand, making them readily accessible to libraries, students, independent scholars, and readers of all ages.

For our initial release we have created seven robust collections to form one the world's most comprehensive catalogs of 18th century works.

*Initial Gale ECCO Print Editions collections include:*

### History and Geography
Rich in titles on English life and social history, this collection spans the world as it was known to eighteenth-century historians and explorers. Titles include a wealth of travel accounts and diaries, histories of nations from throughout the world, and maps and charts of a world that was still being discovered. Students of the War of American Independence will find fascinating accounts from the British side of conflict.

## Social Science

Delve into what it was like to live during the eighteenth century by reading the first-hand accounts of everyday people, including city dwellers and farmers, businessmen and bankers, artisans and merchants, artists and their patrons, politicians and their constituents. Original texts make the American, French, and Industrial revolutions vividly contemporary.

## Medicine, Science and Technology

Medical theory and practice of the 1700s developed rapidly, as is evidenced by the extensive collection, which includes descriptions of diseases, their conditions, and treatments. Books on science and technology, agriculture, military technology, natural philosophy, even cookbooks, are all contained here.

## Literature and Language

Western literary study flows out of eighteenth-century works by Alexander Pope, Daniel Defoe, Henry Fielding, Frances Burney, Denis Diderot, Johann Gottfried Herder, Johann Wolfgang von Goethe, and others. Experience the birth of the modern novel, or compare the development of language using dictionaries and grammar discourses.

## Religion and Philosophy

The Age of Enlightenment profoundly enriched religious and philosophical understanding and continues to influence present-day thinking. Works collected here include masterpieces by David Hume, Immanuel Kant, and Jean-Jacques Rousseau, as well as religious sermons and moral debates on the issues of the day, such as the slave trade. The Age of Reason saw conflict between Protestantism and Catholicism transformed into one between faith and logic -- a debate that continues in the twenty-first century.

## Law and Reference

This collection reveals the history of English common law and Empire law in a vastly changing world of British expansion. Dominating the legal field is the *Commentaries of the Law of England* by Sir William Blackstone, which first appeared in 1765. Reference works such as almanacs and catalogues continue to educate us by revealing the day-to-day workings of society.

## Fine Arts

The eighteenth-century fascination with Greek and Roman antiquity followed the systematic excavation of the ruins at Pompeii and Herculaneum in southern Italy; and after 1750 a neoclassical style dominated all artistic fields. The titles here trace developments in mostly English-language works on painting, sculpture, architecture, music, theater, and other disciplines. Instructional works on musical instruments, catalogs of art objects, comic operas, and more are also included.

## The BiblioLife Network

This project was made possible in part by the BiblioLife Network (BLN), a project aimed at addressing some of the huge challenges facing book preservationists around the world. The BLN includes libraries, library networks, archives, subject matter experts, online communities and library service providers. We believe every book ever published should be available as a high-quality print reproduction; printed on-demand anywhere in the world. This insures the ongoing accessibility of the content and helps generate sustainable revenue for the libraries and organizations that work to preserve these important materials.

The following book is in the "public domain" and represents an authentic reproduction of the text as printed by the original publisher. While we have attempted to accurately maintain the integrity of the original work, there are sometimes problems with the original work or the micro-film from which the books were digitized. This can result in minor errors in reproduction. Possible imperfections include missing and blurred pages, poor pictures, markings and other reproduction issues beyond our control. Because this work is culturally important, we have made it available as part of our commitment to protecting, preserving, and promoting the world's literature.

## GUIDE TO FOLD-OUTS MAPS and OVERSIZED IMAGES

The book you are reading was digitized from microfilm captured over the past thirty to forty years. Years after the creation of the original microfilm, the book was converted to digital files and made available in an online database.

In an online database, page images do not need to conform to the size restrictions found in a printed book. When converting these images back into a printed bound book, the page sizes are standardized in ways that maintain the detail of the original. For large images, such as fold-out maps, the original page image is split into two or more pages

Guidelines used to determine how to split the page image follows:

• Some images are split vertically; large images require vertical and horizontal splits.
• For horizontal splits, the content is split left to right.
• For vertical splits, the content is split from top to bottom.
• For both vertical and horizontal splits, the image is processed from top left to bottom right.

# TWENTY-FOUR VIEWS

IN

# HINDOOSTAN.

*ORIENTAL SCENERY.*

---

# TWENTY-FOUR VIEWS

### IN

# HINDOOSTAN,

### TAKEN IN THE YEARS 1789 AND 1790,

##### DRAWN AND ENGRAVED BY

# *THOMAS DANIELL,*

##### AND, WITH PERMISSION,

#### RESPECTFULLY DEDICATED TO

## THE HONOURABLE COURT OF DIRECTORS

##### OF THE

## *EAST INDIA COMPANY*

LONDON, MARCH 1, 1795

# EASTERN GATE OF THE JUMMA MUSJED,

## AT DELHI

This Gate of the Jumma Musjed, or principal place of worſhip of the Mahommedans, was erected, together with the Moſque, by the Emperor Shah Jehan in the year 1650 of the Chriſtian era. The materials are of reddiſh ſtone, brought from the neighbouring Mewat hills, and white Caſhmerian marble The ſpires on the ſmall domes are gilt The folding doors are covered with braſs, very neatly ornamented with a regular deſign in baſſo relievo. The whole is of excellent workmanſhip.

The figures, &c repreſent the Killadar, or governor of the fort, with his uſual attendants

Delhi, the reſidence of the Mogul Emperor, is about nine hundred and ſeventy-ſix

# HINDOO TEMPLES AT BINDRABUND,

## ON THE RIVER JUMNA.

THESE Edifices are built of ftone, in the ftyle of ancient Hindoo architecture· one of them is ftill in tolerable prefervation, it appears to have been built with confiderable care, and the ornamental parts are executed in a very good tafte. The bafement ftory contains the idol Seva, to whom this temple is dedicated

At what period they were erected could not be learnt: indeed, to afcertain the date of any of the Hindoo buildings not merely modern, is exceedingly difficult, and it rarely happens any information can be obtained deferving credit.

Bindrabund is about feventy miles fouthward of Delhi, a large, populous, and very ancient town, principally inhabited by Hindoos.

## N° III

# THE COTSEA BHAUG,

### ON THE RIVER JUMNA,

### AT DELHI.

COTSEA BHAUG, fo called from the *bhaug,* or garden, within this quadrangular building, which was erected by the Cotfea Begum, a Mahommedan lady, in the reign of the Emperor Akbar, about two hundred years fince. It is built with ftone, and covered in part with ftucco of a very durable nature  The apartments receive light principally from the garden fide, excepting the octangular projections at the angles.  The roof is fmoothly terraced, and commands a fine view of the city of Delhi and the river Jumna  The garden, in which beds of flowers and fountains are interfperfed, is laid out in ftraight walks paved with freeftone.  On the fouth fide, adjoining the outer wall, there is a mofque, and on the north is the grand entrance to the Cotfea Bhaug

# Nº IV.

## RUINS AT THE ANCIENT CITY OF GOUR,

### FORMERLY ON THE BANKS OF THE RIVER GANGES

Of Gour there are accounts fo early as three hundred and fifty years before the Chriftian era, it has been the capital of Bengal three feveral times, and as often deferted. This city appears by its fcattered remains to have been of very confiderable extent, though at this time it is nearly overgrown with jungle (i e. reeds, thorns, and clofe underwood). The Ganges, which formerly wafhed its walls, now runs eight or ten miles to the weftward of it.

By the appearance of the adjoining wall it is probable this gate belonged to the fort.

Gour ftands on the eaftern bank of the river, and is diftant from Calcutta about one hundred and feventy miles, north.

## N° V.

## RAJE GAUT,

### THE PRINCIPAL ROAD UP TO ROTAS GHUR,
### BAHAR.

ROTAS GHUR is the moſt conſiderable hill fort in this part of India, it is naturally of great ſtrength, and the weaker parts have been aſſiſted by very ſtrong works. Within the fort are the remains of ſeveral Hindoo temples, Mahommedan moſques, a palace, and other public buildings, in which frequent examples of excellent architecture occur The mountain on the top of which it ſtands is ſaid to be above eight hundred feet in height, and more than twenty miles in circumference The river Soane waſhes its baſe to the ſouth eaſt.

Rotas Ghur is about three hundred and forty miles N. W from Calcutta

# N° VI

## THE CHALEES SATOON,

### ON THE JUMNA SIDE OF THE FORT OF ALLAHABAD.

THE Chalees Satoon, or the *Forty Pillars*, is a pavilion attached to the palace of Allahabad, and was erected by the Emperor Akbar It is built of grey granite and freestone

The fort of Allahabad is favourably situated on the point where the rivers Ganges and Jumna unite The numerous vessels to be seen on these rivers, particular.y on the former, give great spirit to the scenery.

The buildings in general here are in the grandest style of Mahommedan architecture.

Allahabad is five hundred and fifty miles N. W from Calcutta, and eighty-three westward from Benares.

# N° VII.

## REMAINS OF AN ANCIENT BUILDING
### NEAR FIROZ SHAH'S COTILLAH,
#### AT DELHI

THE plan of the outer wall is quadrangular, with round towers at the angles, and in the centre stands the durbar, or hall of audience. This building is very much in ruin, as well as those surrounding it for many miles It is distant from the fort of Shah Jehanabad, or modern Delhi, about three miles.

## Nº VIII.

## PART OF THE PALACE

### IN THE FORT OF ALLAHABAD

THIS building, compofed chiefly of free-ftone, was erected by the Emperor Akbar, the pillars are richly ornamented, and the whole executed in a mafterly ftyle In the centre of the terrace, on the top of the building, ftood a turret of white marble, very elegantly finifhed, which was taken down by order of the Nabob of Oud, and fent to Lucknow in the year 1789.

Since this view was drawn, the Nabob of Oud has ordered the whole of the building to be taken down and carried to Lucknow, with the intention, it is faid, to be again erected in that city a circumftance much to be lamented, as the abilities of modern work-men are by no means equal to a tafk fo dif-ficult and fo extraordinary as the feparating, removing, and again uniting the materials of fo excellent a ftructure.

# N° IX

## THE GATE

### LEADING TO THE MAUSOLEUM OF THE EMPEROR AKBAR, AT SECUNDRA, NEAR AGRA.

THIS magnificent Gate is built of reddish freeftone, and the ornamental part inlaid with ftones of various colours. The minars are of white marble, executed with great neatnefs, originally they were crowned with turrets, which have been deftroyed by lightning. The maufoleum within the garden, compofed of the fame materials, has a ftriking and grand effect, at the top of which, on the terrace, is placed the body of the Emperor, enclofed in a white marble tomb, elegantly ornamented.

Secundra is nine miles from Agra, and about one hundred and twenty-eight fouthward of Delhi.

## N° X.

# PART OF THE CITY OF PATNA,

## ON THE RIVER GANGES

THE large and populous City of Patna is in the province of Bahar    The gauts, or fteps leading up from the river, are very numerous here, and are intended for the advantage of merchandife, as well as the convenience of the Hindoos, whofe religious duties oblige them frequently to perform ablutions in the facred river Ganges

The larger building is the houfe of an Hindoo merchant, and is an example of the general ftyle of buildings on the river fide inhabited by men of that clafs

Patna is four hundred miles N W. of Calcutta

# Nº XI.

## AN ANCIENT HINDOO TEMPLE

### IN THE FORT OF ROTAS.

THIS building, compofed of grey granite, is of fingular conftruction, and has the appearance of great antiquity. The Hindoos, who formerly preferred elevated places for their temples, could not, it would feem, refift the temptation of building in this place, the fituation being delightful, and water and wood, with every other convenience, abundant.

## N° XII

# THE MAUSOLEUM OF MUCDOOM SHAH DOWLUT,

### AT MONEAH, ON THE RIVER SOANE.

THE Mausoleum of Mucdoom Shah is celebrated for its beauty, it was built at the beginning of the sixteenth century, in the reign of the Emperor Jehangire, by Mucdoom Shah, who was chief of the district.

A small but neat mosque is attached to it, as well as a very considerable tank and garden.

The town Moneah is situated on the east bank of the Soane, nearly at the junction of that river with the Ganges, about twenty-five miles westward from the city of Patna.

## N° XIII.

## PART OF THE FORT BUILT BY THE EMPEROR SHERE SHAH,

### AT DELHI.

SHERE SHAH'S FORT, as it is generally called, is remarkable for the ftrength of its walls; within which there are the remains of a large mofque of excellent workmanfhip, with many other buildings, but the whole are very much in ruins. It is fituated without the walls of Shah Jehanabad, or modern Delhi, which is the third city of that name, the moft ancient occupied a rifing ground about twelve miles S.W from the prefent city, the fecond, as well as the laft, is on the S.W banks of the river Jumna

# N° XIV.

## RAMNUGUR,

NEARLY OPPOSITE BERNARES, ON THE
RIVER GANGES

RAMNUGUR is a fort built by Rajah Bulwunt
Sing, and confiderably improved by his fon
Cheyt Sing. Near to this fort the latter
Rajah began to erect a temple for the Hindoo
worfhip, the bafement ftory only of which is
completed, it is of freeftone, and much ad-
mired for the richnefs of its ornamental
parts, and the very extraordinary degree of
fharpnefs and precifion in their execution.

Ramnugur is about three miles above
Bernares.

## Nº XV.

# THE SACRED TREE AT GYAH,
### IN THE PROVINCE OF BAHAR

By the natives this favourite Tree is called the *Bhur*, and by Europeans the *Banyan* It is a species of the fig, and bears a small red fruit In every village they are to be met with. Small temples are usually built under them, where frequently may be observed fragments of mutilated idols, the work of Mahommedan intolerance, which are again often collected by the patient Hindoos, and, though defaced, are still regarded with veneration

This Tree, the Bramins assure the people, proceeds from another more sacred one, which is growing within a very ancient temple, under ground, in the fort of Allahabad, and, notwithstanding the distance is not less than two hundred miles, the story obtains an easy belief from credulous devotees, who cheerfully pay the sacred fee that admits them to a ceremonial adoration of it

Gyah is near three hundred miles N W. from Calcutta.

# N° XVI.

## DUSASUMADE GAUT, AT BERNARES,

### ON THE RIVER GANGES.

THE Gauts at Bernares are the moft confiderable of any on the Ganges. The houfes on the river fide are occupied for the greater part by religious Hindoos. Vaft multitudes of devotees, and others, refort to this city to perform penance, and tranfact mercantile affairs. An opinion prevails amongft them, that drawing their laft breath at Coffi (the ancient name of this holy city) is a circumftance much in favour of their enjoyment of future happinefs.

Bernares is four hundred and fixty miles N W from Calcutta, on the eaftern bank of the river.

## N° XVII.

## MAUSOLEUM OF SULTAN CHUSERO,

### NEAR ALLAHABAD

SULTAN CHUSERO was the fon of the Emperor Jehangire. His tomb is fituated amidft trees of confiderable magnitude in a handfome garden, laid out in the Hindooftan tafte, with paved walks, avenues, and fountains

The Maufoleum is built of freeftone upon a paved terrace, and the whole has a grand effect.

Sultan Chufero died in the year 1621.

## THE PRINCIPAL GATE LEADING TO THE TAJE MAH'L,

### AT AGRA.

THIS Gate is of red ftone and white marble, elegantly ornamented. The fpandels over the arches are decorated with foliage of various coloured ftones inlaid. The Taje Mah'l is a maufoleum of white marble, built by the Emperor Shah Jehan, in the year 1631, for his favourite Queen, and is confidered by the natives as the moft beautiful work of the kind in Hindooftan  The Emperor alfo lies interred here.

The fpace between the gate and the tomb is converted into a garden, with avenues of trees, fountains, beds of flowers, &c The river Jumna wafhes the lofty walls of the terrace on which this celebrated building ftands.

Agra is diftant from Delhi fouthward about one hundred and thirty-feven miles.

## N° XIX.

## HINDOO TEMPLES AT AGOUREE,

### ON THE RIVER SOANE, BAHAR

AGOUREE is pleaſantly ſituated on the river Soane, ſurrounded with hills well covered with wood   In this place are many Hindoo temples, and alſo a ſmall fort, which make a very picturefque appearance from the river.

Agouree is a place of worſhip of the greateſt antiquity, which is obvious from the fragments of ſculptured idols frequently to be met with there   The village at preſent is not very confiderable

The large tree in this view is the Banyan, or Bhur.

Agouree is about fifty miles ſouth from Chunar Gur.

# N° XX.

## VIEW OF PART OF ROTAS GHUR,

### IN BAHAR.

THIS view of Rotas Ghur was taken nearly at the top of the mountain within the works. A temple of the Hindoos, with a considerable flight of steps, formerly crowned the eminence on the left, the upper part of which has been thrown down by the Mahommedans, who erected a mosque near to it, and which in its turn is also become a ruin No inhabitants are now to be found within the extensive walls of this magnificent fortress.

There are two gauts, or ways of ascent, to the fort, which are made tolerably easy by stone steps, the one called *Raje Gaut* (which is the superior), the other *Acbarpore Gaut*, which takes its name from the village of Acbarpore, near the foot of the mountain.

## N° XXI

## HINDOO TEMPLE NEAR CURRAH,

### ON THE EASTERN BANK OF THE
### RIVER GANGES.

CURRAH was formerly a very confiderable town, about one hundred miles above the city of Bernares, on the oppofite fide of the river. This temple, although built for the worfhip of Hindoo idols, is almoft wholly in the Mahommedan ftyle of defign, as indeed are many other modern Hindoo temples.

The banks of the Ganges are here very lofty, fteep, and picturefque, but are fubject to confiderable alterations in the rainy feafon, as the river then rifes to the height of thirty feet.

N° XXII.

# MAUSOLEUM OF SULTAN PURVEIZ,

### NEAR ALLAHABAD.

THE remains of Sultan Purveiz, the fon of
the Emperor Jehangire, were here depofited
about the year 1626. The fimplicity of the
general defign of this Maufoleum, with its
judicious and well-executed decorations,
rank it among the moft correct examples of
Indian architecture. By time and neglect,
however, this building is much impaired
The dome was originally covered with glaz-
ed tiles, fo formed and difpofed, as to pro-
duce a very rich effect, and of which there
are many beautiful examples ftill remaining
at Agra and Delhi

This Maufoleum is in the fame garden,
near to that of his brother Sultan Chufero.

## N° XXIII.

# THE JUMMAH MUSJED,

### AT DELHI.

THE Jummah Musjed, or *Friday's Mosque*, is the principal place of religious worship of the followers of the Mahommedan doctrine in India. This edifice was built by the Emperor Shah Jehan, as before mentioned. The domes, and all the other parts which appear white, are of Cashmerian marble, the rest of red stone procured in the neighbourhood of Delhi. In regularity of design and correctness of execution this building is considered of the first class. It is approached by three magnificent gates, one of which is the subject of the first plate of these views.

## Nº XXIV.

## GATE LEADING TO A MUSJED,

### AT CHUNAR GUR.

CHUNAR GUR, formerly an Hindoo fort of considerable consequence, and now in the possession of the East India Company, is situated on the western bank of the Ganges, about four hundred and sixty-nine miles N. W. from Calcutta.

The effect of this gate, at a distance, is grand, from the bold projection of its superior parts, and its ornaments, though numerous, are applied with so much art and discretion, as to form the happiest union of beauty and grandeur.

Printed in the USA
CPSIA information can be obtained
at www.ICGtesting.com
LVHW081914090823
754811LV00010B/406